To Summer,

May the Songs of Christmas
fill your heart with joy
all year long.

Peace & Joy,

Fr Edward Kane

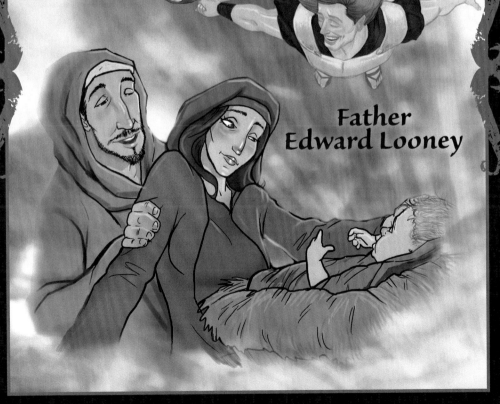

Breakfast in Bethlehem
Father Edward Looney

Illustrated by Jeff West

Cover and book design: Amor Deus Publishing Design Department

For information regarding permission, write to:
Amor Deus Publishing
Attention: Permissions Dept.
4727 North 12th Street
Phoenix, AZ 85014

ISBN 978-1-61956-140-3

Second Edition May 2014
10 9 8 7 6 5 4 3 2

Amor
DEUS
PUBLISHING

First Edition printed June 2013 by Tau Publishing, LLC.

Published and printed in the United States of America by Amor Deus Publishing, an imprint of Vesuvius Press Incorporated.

Dedication:

One day when I was searching through my grandmother's possessions, I happened upon my First Communion pictures. One of the pictures captured me and Sister M. Lipharda Faber, SSND, a religious sister who worked at my home parish. While I never attended Catholic grade school, I had many interactions with Sister Lipharda as an altar server. It is in her loving memory, that I dedicate this book.

The candles are lit.
The church is dark.
I cannot see anything.

I hear church bells ringing.
Ding. Dong. Ding. Dong.
Ding. Dong. Ding. Dong.
Ding. Dong. Ding. Dong.
The bells rang twelve times.
It is midnight.

My mom, dad, brother, sister, and grandparents
are all sitting in a pew at St. Stephen Church.
I hear someone singing:
"The twenty-fifth day of December."

It is Christmas day, Jesus Christ has been born,
and I am at church well past my bedtime.

Every year my family goes to
midnight Mass on Christmas night.

People have done it for many years;
it is a tradition for our family.

After falling asleep for a few minutes, I wake up,
and we are singing a Christmas song,
"O little town of Bethlehem…."
Bethlehem, I remember learning
that is the place where Jesus was born.

The deacon sang to us at the end of Mass.
The song he sang was not a Christmas song.
He sang: "Go and announce the Gospel of the Lord."

Mass went faster than normal.
My mom, dad, brother, sister and I went home,
and Grandpa and Grandma went to their home.

I get to see Grandma and Grandpa
twice in two days because
they are coming over in the morning.
When they arrive they will put their presents
under the tree and after breakfast we will open them.

I was really tired when we got home from Mass. I tried to stay up to see if Santa would eat the cookies and milk my sister Molly and I put out for him. Usually he only takes one bite of the cookie and drinks half of the milk. Like every other year, I fell asleep before Santa came.

While I was sleeping, I had a dream. I dream a lot. I do not remember many dreams, but this one was different, it did not feel like a dream, I thought it was real. I remember every minute and detail of the dream.

I saw an angel and he said to me,
"Come with me to Bethlehem
to see the newborn king!"
I did not know who the king was,
but I followed him.

He took me by the hand and led me to the city called
Bethlehem. On our way to Bethlehem,
I could hear choirs of angels singing,
"Gloria In Excelsis Deo"
In Latin this means
"Glory to God in the Highest."

Once we arrived in Bethlehem I saw a couple and their donkey.

The man was leading the donkey while the woman sat upon it. Her stomach was really big. She was pregnant. Their names were Joseph and Mary, and Mary was getting ready to give birth to their son. They were going to name the baby Jesus.

Nine months earlier, an angel visited Mary and told her she was going to have a baby and that he would be the Son of God. This baby was going to save everyone from their sins.

I watched Joseph knock on the door of a home. I heard him ask if they had an extra room for him and his wife because Mary was ready to give birth to Jesus. The family in the first house refused to let Joseph and Mary inside. Joseph kept walking with the donkey. They found another place, this time an inn. Joseph went inside and asked the man if they had an extra room. He told them there were no rooms but there was space in the stable with the animals.

Mary needed a place to rest, so Joseph gave some money to the innkeeper. They went to the stable and made a place for Mary to rest. In a little while, I heard a baby crying. Mary held the baby in her arms. Joseph looked at Mary holding Jesus in her arms and he smiled because he knew this child was very special.

*J*esus received many visitors. One visit was from three kings who had brought special gifts. When Mary and Joseph opened their gifts, they were confused. They did not understand why the kings brought Jesus incense, gold, and myrrh. Joseph and Mary took the gifts and treasured them.

People from the town of Bethlehem started
to visit the baby Jesus. One of them was a
young boy. He looked about my age.
This little boy played the drum.
As he was walking down the street of Bethlehem
he was playing a song on his drum.

As he walked by the stable where Joseph, Mary, and
Jesus were, the boy with the drum looked in their
direction. The boy started to walk toward Jesus. He
was going to see the newborn king. The boy had no
gift to bring; he could only bring himself and his
music. He came to see the Lord, and played a song for
him on his drum.

The whole town of Bethlehem woke up when they heard the music of the little drummer boy.

One by one, people left their homes, in order to find the boy who was playing music. Above the stable there was a special star, which seemed to guide the people to where Jesus was.
All the people were coming; they were coming joyful and triumphant to adore Christ the Lord.

*T*he line to see Jesus was very long.
When the innkeeper who rented the stable
to Mary and Joseph woke up,
he realized something special had happened.
He felt bad that he could not give them a room and this
baby was receiving so many visitors. He knew people
would be hungry, so he and his wife went into the kitchen
and baked some bread. Once all the loaves were baked,
they gave the bread to every person who was outside. I
could not believe the innkeeper had enough bread to feed
all the people. Everyone who was there, including Mary
and Joseph, were grateful for the gift of the innkeeper, to
make breakfast for everyone in Bethlehem.

The people in Bethlehem began to sing songs to Jesus. While they were singing, my mom and dad started singing too. They did not sing in my dream, but were singing in my room. Every Christmas they would sing songs to wake us up. As I woke up, I was still thinking about Bethlehem, and everything I saw in my dream. What I saw seemed so real. Grandma and Grandpa came over like they do every Christmas morning. I was excited to see them even though I had seen them at Mass last night. Grandpa had gifts for all of us in his arms. I helped him put them under the Christmas tree.

We all sat around the breakfast table. After we prayed, Grandpa asked us what we wanted for Christmas. I thought about what I wanted. I wanted a new game for my Xbox, but after my trip to Bethlehem, I wanted something to remember the dream. I told Grandpa, "I want a picture of the baby Jesus."

Grandpa was surprised, he said, "A picture of Jesus? That is a very nice gift. Jesus is the reason why we celebrate Christmas. He is the reason why we went to Mass last night at midnight." Grandpa then asked, "Why do you want a picture of the baby Jesus?"

I told him, "Last night I had a dream. An angel took me to Bethlehem. He showed me the journey of Joseph and Mary. I saw the baby Jesus, and three kings. There was a boy who played a song for Jesus on his drum. And then everyone from Bethlehem came to see Jesus. The innkeepers where Joseph and Mary were staying made breakfast for everyone who came to visit. They made loaves of bread which were given to everyone.

want a picture of Jesus, because I want to remember this dream. I want to remember the time I saw the child Jesus in Bethlehem."

Grandpa helped me to understand my dream. He told me the gifts the kings brought Jesus were symbolic of Christ as priest, prophet and king. He also said the little drummer boy had no gifts to bring for Jesus, so he brought all that he could. He brought the gift of himself and the gifts God had given him. God gave him the gift of music, and so he gave that gift back to Jesus, the son of God.

The last thing he told me was the bread the innkeepers gave to all the guests, was symbolic of Jesus' gift for the life of the world—his Body and Blood in the Eucharist. The name Bethlehem means "House of Bread." It is in God's house, the church, that ordinary bread becomes the Bread of Life, the Body of Christ. The same Bread of Life that my family received last night at Church and one day I will receive when I make my first Holy Communion. The baby Jesus, for whom everyone brought gifts in Bethlehem, now gives his own life as a gift of food for all those who believe.

When that angel took me to Bethlehem,
I knew my life was going to be different.
Everyone who visited Jesus that night and
morning left with a smile on their face.
They were happy.
When I woke up that morning I was happy too.

That dream made the story of Jesus' birth real to me
and with Grandpa's help I learned something from my
dream.

Sitting around the breakfast table with Grandma, Grandpa, Mom, Dad, my brother and sister, was our own breakfast in Bethlehem.

We were all in the same home because Jesus, the son of God, was born on Christmas day. We opened presents just like Mary and Joseph did when the three kings brought their gifts for Jesus. And now, we knew the only gift we could give Jesus in return on that Christmas morning, was the gift of our lives because Jesus would give the ultimate gift of His life on the cross to save us from our sins.

For as long as I live, I will never forget my breakfast in Bethlehem, because the gift my grandpa put under the tree that morning was a picture of the baby Jesus.

The
End

About the Author:

Fr. Edward Looney was ordained a priest on June 6, 2015. At a young age, he fostered a devotion to the Blessed Mother, which comes alive in his writings. Fr. Looney is a member of the Mariological Society America and publishes regularly in theological journals and online blogs. He is the author of another children's book, "The Story of Sister Adele."

www.edwardlooney.com